PIANO • VOCAL • GUITAR

BROADWAY LOVE SONGS

ISBN 0-7935-1249-2

HL. Hal Leonard Publishing Corporation
7777 West Bluemound Road P.O. Box 13819 Milwaukee, WI 53213

BROADWAY

LOVE SONGS

ALL AT ONCE YOU LOVE HER

(From "PIPE DREAM")

Words by OSCAR HAMMERSTEIN II
Music by RICHARD RODGERS

Slowly, with expression

ALL I ASK OF YOU
(From "THE PHANTOM OF THE OPERA")

Music by ANDREW LLOYD WEBBER
Lyrics by CHARLES HART
Additional Lyrics by RICHARD STILGOE

10

AS ONCE I LOVED YOU
(From "REX")

Words by SHELDON HARNICK
Music by RICHARD RODGERS

ALL OF YOU
(From "SILK STOCKINGS")

Words and Music by
COLE PORTER

Fox trot tempo

mf

no chord

Af- ter watch- ing her ap- peal from ev- 'ry an- gle, ___

___ there's a big ro- man- tic deal I've got to

wan - gle. ___ For I've fal- len for a

ANYONE WOULD LOVE YOU
(From "DESTRY RIDES AGAIN")

Words and Music by
and HAROLD ROME

Simply and earnestly

Speak - ing im - par - tial - ly, not at all per - s'nal - ly, just from a gen - er - al point of view.

mp *p* *legato* *un poco cresc.* *poco rall. e dim.*

BELLS ARE RINGING

(From "BELLS ARE RINGING")

Moderate Waltz

Words and Music by BETTY COMDEN and ADOLPH GREEN
Music by JULE STYNE

Star light, Star bright, I wish for on-ly one thing._____ Will the tel- e- phone ev- er ring _____ for me. _____

Slowly with expression

sight. Me on the town, in some be-witch-ing gown.

But I just wait at the end of the line, As bells are

ring - ing, The bells keep ring - ing, Oh why, oh why can't the

next call be mine._____ mine._____

BEWITCHED
(From "PAL JOEY")

Words by LORENZ HART
Music by RICHARD RODGERS

A BUSHEL AND A PECK

(From "GUYS AND DOLLS")

By FRANK LOESSER

Light Bounce Tempo

DO I LOVE YOU BECAUSE YOU'RE BEAUTIFUL?

(From "CINDERELLA")

Lyrics by OSCAR HAMMERSTEIN II
Music by RICHARD RODGERS

COME RAIN OR COME SHINE
(From "ST. LOUIS WOMAN")

Words by JOHNNY MERCER
Music by HAROLD ARLEN

FALLIN'
(From The Musical "THEY'RE PLAYING OUR SONG")

Lyric by
CAROLE BAYER SAGER

Words by CAROLE BAYER SAGER
Music by MARVIN HAMLISCH

I'm a-fraid to fly, and I don't know why I'm
think by now I'd learn, play with fire you get burned, but

jeal-ous of the peo-ple who are not a-fraid to die. It's
fire can be, oh so warm, that's why I re-turn.

FALLING IN LOVE WITH LOVE

(From "THE BOYS FROM SYRACUSE")

Words by LORENZ HART
Music by RICHARD RODGERS

HELLO, YOUNG LOVERS
(From "THE KING AND I")

Words by OSCAR HAMMERSTEIN II
Music by RICHARD RODGERS

Hel - lo, young lov - ers, who - ev - er you are, I hope your trou - bles are

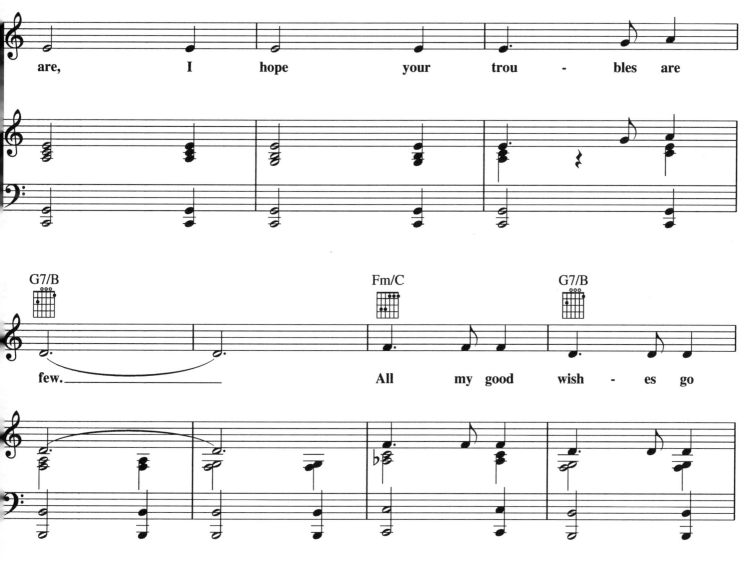

few. _____ All my good wish - es go

THE FIRST MAN YOU REMEMBER

(From "ASPECTS OF LOVE")

Music by ANDREW LLOYD WEBBER
Lyrics by DON BLACK & CHARLES HART

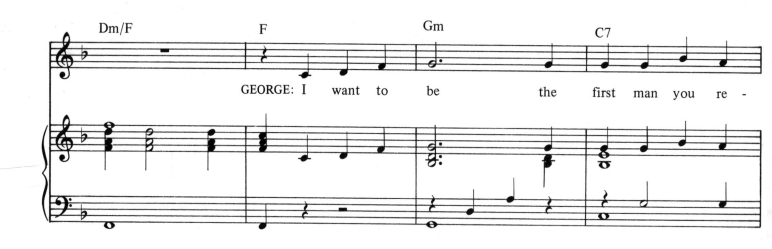

GEORGE: I want to be the first man you re-

mem - ber, I want to be the last man you'll for -

GEORGE: Seems the stars are far be - low us _____

GOODNIGHT MY SOMEONE

(From "THE MUSIC MAN")

Words and Music by
MEREDITH WILLSON

Good-night, My Some-one, good-night, my love. Sleep tight, my some-one, sleep tight, my love, Our star is shin-ing it's bright-est light For good-night, my love for good-

I DO NOT KNOW A DAY
I DID NOT LOVE YOU

(From "TWO BY TWO")

Words by MARTIN CHARNIN
Music by RICHARD RODGERS

I LOVE YOU
(From "SONG OF NORWAY")

Words and Music by ROBERT WRIGHT
and GEORGE FORREST

I KNOW HIM SO WELL
(From "CHESS")

Words and Music by BENNY ANDERSSON,
BJOERN ULVAEUS and TIM RICE

1. No-thing is so good it lasts e - ter-nal-ly, _____
2. Look-ing back I could have played it dif-fer-ent-ly, _____

per-fect si - tu-a-tions must go wrong.
won a few more moments, who can tell.

But this has nev-er yet pre-vent - ed me _____
But it took time to un-der-stand the man. _____

want-ing far too much for far too long.
Now at least I know I know him well. Was-n't it good?

Oh, so good! _____ Oh, so fine! _____ He can't be mine?

Was-n't he fine? _____ Is-n't it mad - ness he can't be mine?

I LOVE MY WIFE

(From "I DO! I DO!")

Words by
TOM JONES

Words by TOM JONES
Music by HARVEY SCHMIDT

strick - en for life. "My son," he said, "Get

back to bed. You hap-pen to love your wife!"

Oth - er men love mov - ie stars, but not I. The

sort you wor-ship from a - far, And I try.

I LOVE YOU
(From "MEXICAN HAYRIDE")

Words and Music by
COLE PORTER

I STILL BELIEVE IN LOVE

(From "THEY'RE PLAYING OUR SONG")

Words by CAROLE BAYER SAGER
Music by MARVIN HAMLISCH

Moderate Rock Ballad

IF EVER I WOULD LEAVE YOU

(From "CAMELOT")

Words by ALAN JAY LERNER
Music by FREDERICK LOEWE

I'LL BE SEEING YOU

(From "RIGHT THIS WAY")

Words and Music by IRVING KAHAL
and SAMMY FAIN

I'VE GROWN ACCUSTOMED TO HER FACE

(From "MY FAIR LADY")

Words by ALAN JAY LERNER
Music by FREDERICK LOEWE

LOVE CHANGES EVERYTHING

(From "ASPECTS OF LOVE")

Music by ANDREW LLOYD WEBBER
Lyrics by DON BLACK and CHARLES HART

LUCKY IN LOVE
(From "GOOD NEWS")

Words and Music by B.G. DeSYLVA,
LEW BROWN and RAY HENDERSON

MY CUP RUNNETH OVER
(From "I DO! I DO!")

Words by TOM JONES
Music by HARVEY SCHMIDT

MY FUNNY VALENTINE

(From "BABES IN ARMS")

Words by LORENZ HART
Music by RICHARD RODGERS

MR. WONDERFUL
(From the Musical "MR. WONDERFUL")

Words and Music by JERRY BOCK,
LARRY HOLOFCENER and GEORGE WEISS

Why this feel - ing? _____ Why this glow? _____

_____ Why the thrill when you say, "Hel - lo!"? _____

ON THE STREET WHERE YOU LIVE
(From "MY FAIR LADY")

Words by ALAN JAY LERNER
Music by FREDERICK LOEWE

NO OTHER LOVE
(From "ME AND JULIET")

Lyrics by OSCAR HAMMERSTEIN
Music By RICHARD RODGE

Moderately

mf

Cm   Cm6   Ab7   G7b5

How far a-way are you?   How man-y lone-ly sighs, dear?

Gb7   F7b5   Bb7   Eb   G7

How man-y weep-ing skies, dear?   How far a-way are you?

Cm   Cm6   Ab7   G7b5

How long have I to go?   How man-y moons to see, dear,

OUR LANGUAGE OF LOVE
(From "IRMA LA DOUCE")

Music by MARGUERITE MONNOT
Original French words by ALEXANDRE BREFFORT
English words by JULIAN MORE,
DAVID HENEKER and MONTY NORMAN

PARIS LOVES LOVERS
(From "SILK STOCKINGS")

Words and Music by
COLE PORTER

Gaze— on those glist-'ning lights be-loward a-bove. Oh, what a night of nights for peo-ple in love. No cit - y but this, my friend, no cit - y I know Gives ro-mance such a chance to grow and grow.

PEOPLE WILL SAY WE'RE IN LOVE

(From "OKLAHOMA!")

Lyrics by OSCAR HAMMERSTEIN II
Music by RICHARD RODGERS

SO IN LOVE
(From "KISS ME, KATE")

Words and Music by COLE PORTER

Strange, dear, _____ but true, dear, _____ When I'm close _____ to you, dear, _____ The

129

SOME ENCHANTED EVENING
(From "SOUTH PACIFIC")

Words by OSCAR HAMMERSTEIN II
Music by RICHARD RODGERS

SUN AND MOON
(From "MISS SAIGON")

Music by CLAUDE-MICHEL SCHÖNBERG
Lyrics by RICHARD MALTBY JR. & ALAIN BOUBLIL
Adapted from original French Lyrics by ALAIN BOUBLIL

SUMMERTIME LOVE
(From "GREENWILLOW")

By FRANK LOESSE[r]

SUNRISE, SUNSET
(From the Musical "FIDDLER ON THE ROOF")

Words by SHELDON HARNIC
Music by JERRY BOC

THERE'S A SMALL HOTEL
(From "ON YOUR TOES")

Words by LORENZ HART
Music by RICHARD RODGERS

There's a small ho-tel With a wish-ing well; I
wish that we were there to-geth-er. _____
There's a brid-al suite; One room bright and neat, Com-

stee - ple bell says, "Good - night, sleep well," we'll

thank the small ho - tel to - geth - er._____

tel._____ We'll creep in - to our lit - tle shell_____ And we will

thank the small ho - tel to - geth - er._____

rit. *L.H.* *mf*

ped.

THINK OF ME
(From "THE PHANTOM OF THE OPERA")

Music by ANDREW LLOYD WEBBER
Lyrics by CHARLES HART
Additional Lyrics by RICHARD STILGOE

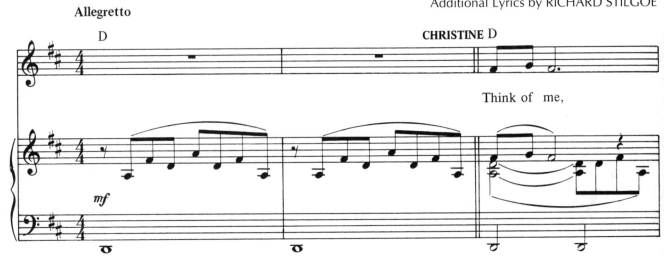

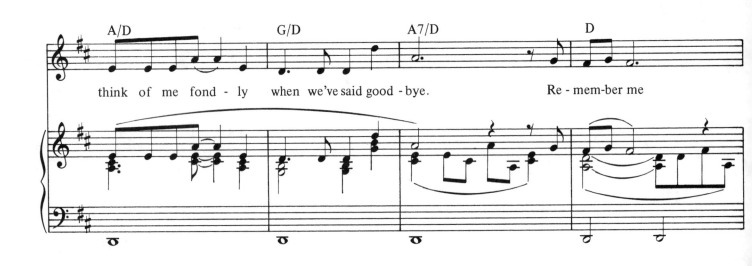

CHRISTINE

me but I re - mem - ber her We nev - er said ___ our love was ev - er - green, ___ or as un - chang - ing as the sea — but please pro - mise me that some - times you will think ah ___ etc... of me!

TILL THERE WAS YOU
(From "THE MUSIC MAN")

Words and Music by
MEREDITH WILLSON

There were bells___ on a hill,___ but I
birds___ in the sky,___ but I

nev - er___ heard them ring - ing,___ No, I nev - er heard them at
nev - er___ saw them wing - ing,___ No, I nev - er saw them at

TOGETHER
(From "GOOD NEWS")

Words and Music by B.G. DeSYLV
RAY HENDERSON and LEW BROW

Moderately Slow

We strolled the lane, To- geth- er

Laughed at the rain, To- geth- er

Sang love's re- frain, To- geth- er. And we'd
We knew

8vb

TOGETHER WHEREVER WE GO
(From "GYPSY")

Words by STEPHEN SONDHEIM
Music by JULE STYNE

TOGETHER FOREVER

(From "I DO! I DO!")

Words by TOM JONES
Music by HARVEY SCHMIDT

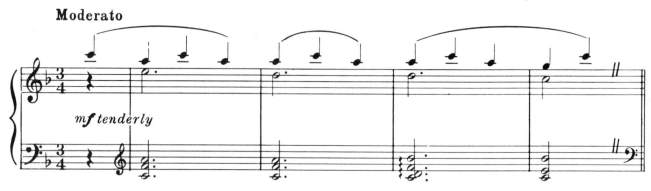

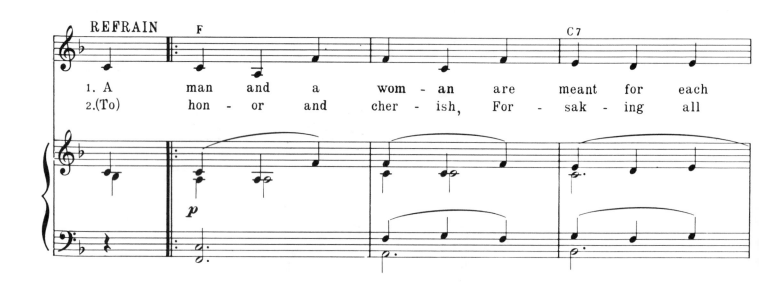

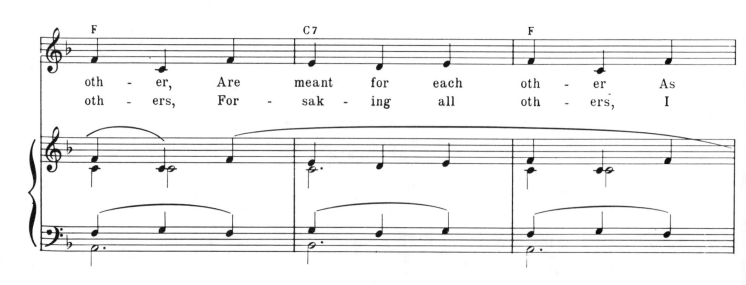

UNEXPECTED SONG
(From "SONG & DANCE")

Music by Andrew Lloyd Webber
Lyrics by Don Black

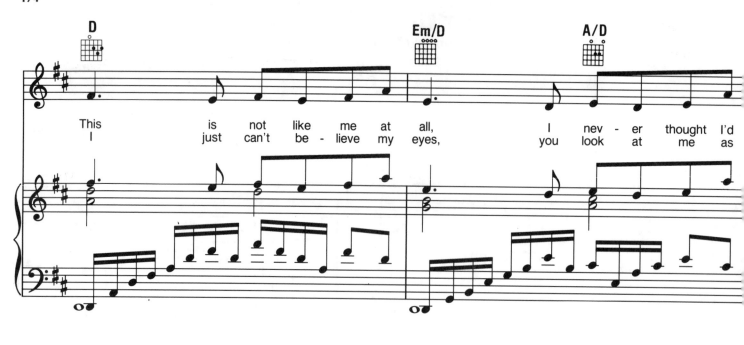

This is not like me at all, I just can't be-lieve my eyes, you nev-er thought I'd

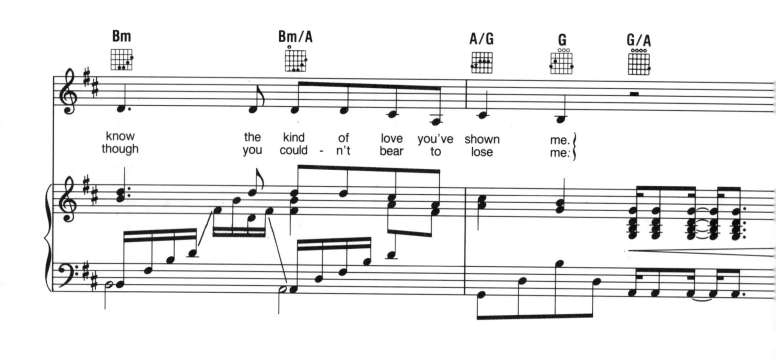

know the kind of love you've shown me.
though you could-n't bear to lose me:

Now no mat-ter where I am, no mat-ter what I do, I see your face ap

pear - ing   like   an un - ex - pect - ed song,   an un - ex - pect - ed

song   that on - ly we are hear - ing.   hear - ing.

I have nev - er felt like this.   For once I'm lost for words,   your smile has real - ly

thrown me. This is not like me at all, I nev-er thought I'd

know the kind of love you've shown me. Now no mat-ter where I

am, no mat-ter what I do, I see your face ap-pear-ing like an un-ex-pect-ed

song, an un-ex-pect-ed song that on-ly we are hear-ing.

Like an un-ex-pect-ed song, an un-ex-pect-ed song that on-ly we are

hear-ing.

WE KISS IN A SHADOW

(From "THE KING AND I")

Words by OSCAR HAMMERSTEIN
Music by RICHARD RODGERS

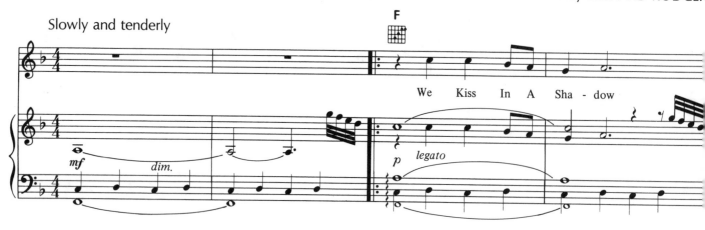

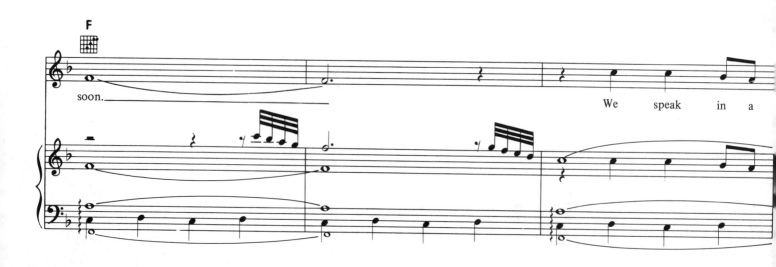

WE MAKE A BEAUTIFUL PAIR

(From "SHENANDOAH")

Lyrics by PETER UDELL
Music by GARY GELD

185

YOU ARE BEAUTIFUL

(From "FLOWER DRUM SONG")

Words by OSCAR HAMMERSTEIN
Music by RICHARD RODGERS

WHY DID I CHOOSE YOU?

(From "THE YEARLING")

Lyric by HERBERT MARTIN
Music by MICHAEL LEONARD